Also by Lyn

I Am a Rock God! :
Adult Coloring, Activity, & Songwriting Book for Musicians
(with inspiring lyrics and original poems co-written by Jacob Wier)

I Am a Rock Goddess! :
Adult Coloring, Activity, & Songwriting Book for Musicians
(with inspiring lyrics and original poems co-written by Jacob Wier)

─────●━●●━●─────

For inquiries and permissions contact the publisher at:
lmf.limitless.muses@gmail.com

Or message and follow us on Facebook:
https://www.facebook.com/LMFLimitlessMuses

Or find and follow us on Author Central for future products and updates.

Kindly leave a review. It helps improve our products.

─────●━●●━●─────

For inquiries and permissions contact the illustrator at:
(231)-878-8335

Ms. Kushion's artwork is available at:
Tawas Bay Art Gallery
East Tawas, MI 48730

WHY BE EYE CANDY
WHEN YOU CAN BE SOUL FOOD?

by
Lynette Feeley

Illustrations by
Carol Gazso Kushion

Edited by
Maria A Arana

Author Copyright 2023 Lynette Feeley
Why Be Eye Candy When You Can Be Soul Food?
First Edition Fall of *2023*

Illustrator Copyright 2023 Carol Gazso Kushion

Book cover illustrations Copyright 2023 Carol Gazso Kushion

Book cover design Copyright 2023
Carol Gazso Kushion & LMF Limitless Muses, LLC

Editing by Maria A. Arana: aranaeditingservices.com

This is a work of fiction based on events or observations in the
author's life. The author has given every effort to remove identifying factors from
her work. To this end, any real-life depictions are purely coincidental.

ISBN: 9798867203986

Published in the fall of 2023 in the USA
by
LMF Limitless Muses, LLC.

To my fellow empaths trying to find their footing in life:
Look within and know that you are enough in this moment.
Put your best foot forward. All is in divine order.
The rest will work out with time.

—Lynette Feeley

With heartfelt appreciation to the Flint Institute of Art (FIA), who welcomed my third-grade self to explore and embrace her creative passions in the summer of 1963.

—Carol Gazso Kushion

Contents

Acknowledgments

Lynette Feeley—I would like to express infinite gratitude to Carol Gazso Kushion, my former, favorite (choir) teacher, director, and humanitarian extraordinaire. Your translation of my words into visual artistry is a thing of sheer beauty. We have created something truly special that shows the limitless possibilities when creative minds come together. A special thank you to Maria Arana at aranaeditingservices.com for her friendship, insight, creative expression, and eagle-eye prowess. You help me put my best foot forward in my life and work. To my loved ones across the veil: You are greatly missed and inspire me to live this life to the fullest. You are ever-present in all of my creative endeavors. To my family, I adore you above all things. I am so grateful that we get to do this thing called life together. To my sisters, thank you for encouraging me to create a product worthy of public viewing. To Michele Newton, Denise Shute (my forever peanut buddy), and Martha Gaye Mathis, thank you for your unconditional friendship and for inspiring me to stay true to my heart. A special thank you to Jennifer Feeley, for telling me to get published elsewhere—you planted the seed, and now here is the sprout!

"Alaska," "Chocolate Makes Her Feel Better," "Fade to Black," and "Wide Awake" first appeared in previous versions in Lyceum The Literary & Fine Arts Journal published by The University of Michigan-Dearborn.

"Lightsome Things" was created from (part of line 19 and all of line 21) "Butterflies Are Lightsome Things," published in Not Written Words by Zephyr Press/mccm creations, 2016. "The Stargazing Cat" was inspired by the poem "The Cat in the Forbidden City Gazes at Stars," published in Carnival of Animals: Xi Xi's Animal Poems by CUHK Press, 2022. Both poems were written by Xi Xi and translated from the Chinese by Jennifer Feeley. Sadly, Xi Xi passed away on December 18, 2022. She was a literary behemoth, especially for Hong Kong, and my sister's thoughtful translations into English diversified my interests and allowed me to appreciate this prolific author and my sister's profound love for her body of work. These poems inspired me to write my two-poem collection titled Xi Xi Pro Memoria as a tribute to my sister (and our then recently late mother), and to pay my respects to Xi Xi and her significant contributions to the literary world. According to the online Merriam-Webster Dictionary, "pro memoria" is rooted in Latin entomology and means "for the sake of memory."

"Dreamer" previously appeared in I Am a Rock Goddess! :Adult Coloring, Activity, & Songwriting Book for Musicians by Jacob Wier and Lynette Feeley.

I paid homage to E.E. Cummings in this collection because he is the first (and favorite) poet who inspired me to realize that words could be elevated into works of art. It only made sense to include this tribute in my first collection. Cummings had a profound influence on my early roots and how I chose to express myself creatively.

Carol Gazso Kushion—My sincere thanks to Lynette Feeley for inviting me to collaborate with her on this worthy and insightful project.

Author's Note

To me, poems (like lyrics) are photographic snapshots of the mind's eye capturing fleeting thoughts at any given moment. These still lives might depict an event, mood, tone, or an observation. The poems in this collection are the best still lives my brain has captured spanning three decades. They tell tales of love, jilted love, self-love, angst, and joy. These works germinated from seeds of truth and grew into a cinematic display of both confessional honesty and thematic fiction. When I string together ideas, they accompany music and visual scenery in my imagination. I feel fortunate to have teamed up with Ms. Kushion, (a true musician and artist) on this project. Our creative visions were closely aligned throughout this process and it often felt like we were extensions of each other. I hope her visual translations of my words on these pages help you compose your own truths and inspire you to bring your artistic visions, in whatever form, to life.

A note about The Stargazing Cat, the pluralization of "ether"(pg. 47, line 5) is not a typo. It is a creative ploy because I like choices. It's okay to say "heaven" or "heavens." We are also given the option to capitalize the word "heaven." Thus, I see no reason why we cannot be given the option to travel into the "ethers" to discover the many places and spaces that undoubtedly exist in the great beyond, if we so desire.

Lynette Feeley
October 2023

Illustrator's Note

I found the opportunity to collaborate with Lynette on her poetry collection quite freeing. Creating a narrowed vision from her words allowed me to broaden and vary my stroke, style, and medium with each stand-alone poem. As with my gallery art, I invest days envisioning a cluster of poems, and when my mind's eye composes a composition that resonates with Lynette's words, it only takes minutes to sketch that composition on paper. The rest is simply choosing a pencil, pen, or brush.

Carol Gazso Kushion
November 2023

Publisher's Note

The publisher abandoned traditional publishing norms for this project. We think of poetry like words on steroids. Each poem depicts imagery unique to the previous one. Poems don't require shelving like a traditional book holding thousands of words (books are masterpieces in their own right). Instead, they are works of art to display on coffee tables, desks, and in waiting rooms and galleries. Like songs, poems can be lyrical. They make eye-catching and thought-provoking gifts. And like art, they are unique conversation pieces. Therefore, we feel poetry requires elevated formatting. To this end, we changed the title headings font from 14 point to 16 point. The poems were not flushed left but centered. This ploy helped happy accidental imagery like "Miracles," "Rain Vows," and "Delicate Flowers" to pop on the page. We used a thin line in the margins to tie in the poems with the artwork and to evoke the feeling that each poem is also a work of art (Thanks, Ms. Kushion!) We centered shorter poems to better align with the illustrations. We hope you enjoy this artistic endeavor.

The publisher owns a commercial license to publish graphic designs and fonts from Creative Fabrica and Canva. We utilized these tools to ready the illustrations for publication and supplement them where necessary, for example, the butterflies in flight on the cover, and the tiny flowers on the filler pages. All remaining doodles and drawings are under the sole Copyright and ownership of the artist, Carol Gazso Kushion. Fonts used were Georgia Pro Condensed, Railey, Sunday and in "The Recycling" only, Cristik.

LMF Limitless Muses

SELF-REFLECTION

Soul Food

Why be eye candy when you can be soul food?
Cleanse your palate and elevate your mood

A peppery tongue can set words apart
While a sweet persona tends to matters of the heart

A cayenne mind can sharpen the wits
But nothing has substance like a bowlful of grits

A salty disposition of chutzpah and gumbo
Can weed through most of life's mumbo jumbo

And a strong-garlic mind rooted in culture
Will stave off any energy vulture

A healthy dose of earthy cornbread
Can keep you grounded—get you outta your head

Marzipan is pretty but comes on thick
While a petite praline can level out quick

A truffle is exquisite at the end of the day
But it won't soothe the soul
Like a cup of chicory coffee and a warm beignet

And if you fill yourself up with a savory étouffée
Your heart and soul will never lead you astray

Milestones

Milestones, milestones,
How to tell the weight of these bones—
Shall I poke them with a stick?
No prod could scratch the surface that my essence depicts

Milestones, milestones,
How to tell the weight of these bones—
Will Sonar acquiesce?
No acoustic pulse will sound at the bottom
Of this Mariana Trench

Milestones, milestones,
How to tell the weight of these bones—
Would a scale educe the stat?
Nominal is far too ordinary,
These bones can't be labeled by this thing or that

An ordinal scale won't do on the whole,
What would rank first, my heart or my soul?

With the interval scale,
How to subtract the difference
Between then and now in equal measure?
Time is a vice that no one escapes, and we must treasure

Can we surmise a life by mean, median, and mode
Without compromising our moral code?
I'm bold. I'm stubborn. I'm curious—to the core!
For every road less traveled, there's a new one to explore

Life lessons are often cloaked in the same clothing twice
But these milestones, immeasurable by any scale,
Are too infinite to suffice

Airplane

Majestic-massive-motor-beast jettisons the clouds—
Inherits the wind
Nothing audible, but the shattering sound barrier
Echolalic like lightning's thunder
I too have left the clouds behind me
I want to ride the winds and conquer them
Like this beast does before me—
Perhaps within me

As a child, clouds seemed like ethereal angels
Enshrouding my cotton candy
Dreams in earthly delights
At times, the cumulus wonders
Appeared as fanciful shapes—
A bunny or a ghostly pony
The child within me grows
Not as a weed on a hot summer's day
But as an unseemly distance between lovers
(Creeping upon you)
Before the dance has ended

For now, I leave it all behind me
And seek great escape for a moment
Or maybe two
It's an incessant circle:
The thrill of taking off!
The harsh-cold reality of landing too fast—
Perhaps too soon
And the coming down is instantaneous and eye-opening
Perhaps a little wider than one could anticipate or even desire

An Economy of Words

Words are like jesters
They tease and joke
But if sharpened too much,
They painfully poke
Words form trains
To keep you on track
Words are not boomerangs
You can never take them back
Sometimes words are better said
And sometimes they are not
Maybe sometime we can get together
And talk about diddly-squat

Forgiveness

If you admit wrongdoing and are remorseful,
Then forgiveness may follow
If your rightness puts another to shame but does not boast,
there could be forgiveness in that
But to forgive someone who shows no remorse,
who flaunts their rightness in our faces,
That is living in the light
It's no easy task, but it makes us whole and at peace

The Power of Choice

Strength doesn't come without,
It comes from within
I am not my job
Or what others might think of me
I alone can make key decisions that empower me
And the power of choice will always be mine
I can ask another to decide
And it absolves me of consequence
But the choice to relinquish my power
Remains my responsibility
I decide what is best for me
After all, nobody knows me like I do
I will do my best to make good choices
Designed to serve my highest self
And the greater good, as I see fit
I will honor my choices and
Know that I have made the wisest decisions
With the knowledge I possess at this time
I will follow the flow of life,
Wherever it may lead,
And know that I am armed with the divine power
Within me to make things possible
Regardless of my current life stage,
I control the narrative
It's never too late to change
Or blossom into who I wish to become

Be an Observer

Be an observer of all things
The world doesn't need another critic
There is no greater judge or jury
Than the voice in our head
Telling us we are not enough
Or that we somehow fall short
You don't need to own what someone
Else says or thinks of you
Judgments reveal more of the giver
Than the receiver
It takes courage and strength
To display kindness in a harsh world
People who reject the opinions of others
Are uncertain of their own beliefs
You may believe what is in your best interest
And I will believe what is right for my own heart
It is okay to agree to disagree
It doesn't matter if you fit in
As long as you stand out
Be outstanding in your own right
And the people whose opinions really matter
Will look up to you

Dreamer

A dream will never come true
Unless you awaken
Authenticity won't shine through
If you try to fake it
Be honest and sincere
Never give in to fear
Let humility be your guide
And you soon will make it

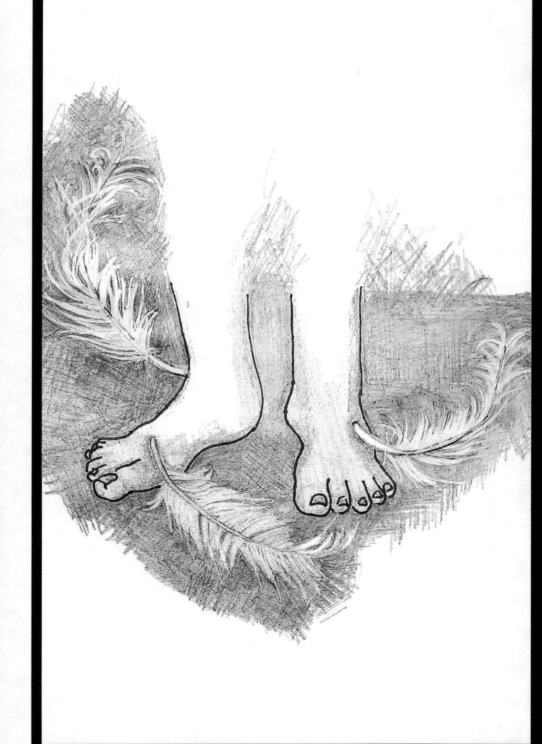

Miracles

People try so hard to explain away miracles
I'd rather believe in miracles and explain away reality
Life is like an iceberg; a quarter is on the surface
And the majority is what you can't see
Angels hold
Blueprints
To our life's plan
All we need to do
Is ask for divine guidance
And reach out a loving hand
Sometimes the lesson is bitter
Other times, the lesson is sweet
But we are never alone in life's
Classroom when we have angels
At our feet

Love
from the
Center
of who you
are.
Romans 12:9

Higher Self

And above all else, love yourself—
For the unconditional heart can never feel dejected
Whisper sweet nothings into your ear
Nothing sounds as melodic as the essence of you
Tell your spirit that it is free
To dance in moonlit waterfalls
Embrace yourself and know that
Pools of judgment merely reflect
The prejudice of others
You alone control
The water's ebb and flow

Allow childlike expression:
Pick flowers
Roll in leaves
Swing to the highest star
And always keep your face toward the sun

Accept your spirit as it is in this moment—
With all of its hopes, fears, and flaws
For light travels faster than sound
And yesterday's seeds of doubt
Sprout tomorrow's growth

If nothing else,
Sit silently with animals, observing nature
And forgive yourself for being human

Wide Awake

The night beside the lava lamp was blissful
I was an evening primrose ripe for the picking
The blue-molten light threw our shadows on the wall
Did they share our sensuality?
Shadows never tell
They sleep content in the dark
But I know we are moments away from dawn
The cock crows and your slender figure
Saunters to the window in stoic silence
Pulling up the shade,
You envelop me in rays of sunlight
Dreams and shadows distanced
I sit solemnly, wide awake

Fade To Black

Hurriedly, we file out of the theater
Into the crisp night air
Tired sun, nodding off,
Lays her head on a pillowed horizon
Inside the frost-misted car,
You are ice waiting to be thawed
My lips grow terse, as I blow
Hot air rings into your frigid soul
Fingers squeak and avidly trace the
Same figure eights on your frozen heart
Our eyes lock briefly then turn peripheral
As we fumble through naked awareness
My mind fades to black, and
I watch old reruns of our
Lovemaking in my head:
Often a playful comedy
Occasionally a short fiction
Sometimes a fantasy
Frequently a sleeper. . .
Splicing recall, the engine drones
As I shift in my chilled leather seat
And you are a silent film
Too many decibels for my fragile ears
The sun has made her final cut—
She is our curtain call
We bow our heads
And take our licorice in silence

The Home Run Hitter

Being fond of commitment, honesty, and respect
I was never one to play the field
Stealing all four bases at once
Sliding into the security of the ho-oh!-ome plate
Oblivious to all other players
One on one is more my sport
I'd rather be insecure and independent
For all the right reasons
Then be secure and dependent
For all the wrong—
A game, these days,
Not so far out in left field

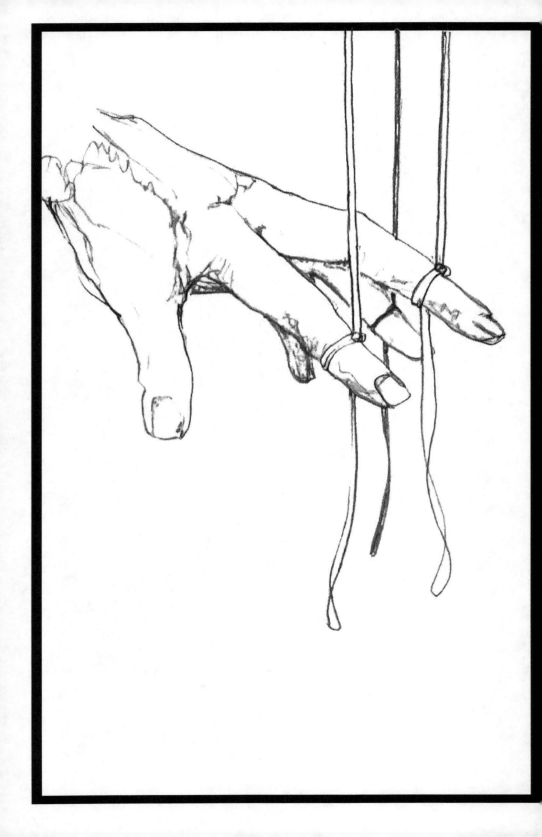

The Puppeteer

Oh, my beloved puppeteer,
You self-indulged young being
Are you feeling rather boastful now
That I dangle from your string?

Let me bow and thank you kindly
Shall I do a little dance?
Anything to keep me off your shelf
Do you think I stand a chance?

For my joints are getting dusty
My clothes are wearing thin
My heart's a little rusty,
Do you care for the shape I'm in?

My master doesn't listen
He heeds not what I say
He doesn't seem to want me
Yet he keeps me on display
It's getting rather lonely
And my mind's begun to fray
I've waited here so very long
I do not wish to stay. . .

But wait— I see another puppet getting tossed my way!
The eyes and hands I recognize from many moons ago
His face looks fairly frazzled and he hangs his head real low
His eyes are worn and weary now that he knows this awful thing
My master's finally learning how to dangle from a lover's string

Escape Room

Long ago, we entered a room of adventure
Stricken by our curiosities, we got lost in a hall of mirrors
Our minds were engaged in mutual discovery
We were enamored with the thrill of mystery
We were closer then—
We were strangers
And now intimacy is the wedge
That divides this chasm further between us
Mirrored memories seem warped and distorted
You sit in the pit of my stomach
Like a simmered roast on Christmas morning
And your self-indulgence tastes rancid on my tongue

My hindsight is 20/40
But you saw this coming
We drained the marrow from life
Bit off more than we could chew
And now, we are left with the bone—
I choke
You bury
Your belly is full
And my hunger can't be satiated

You escape the room with stealth and haste
I lack the courage to place my hand on the door
Are you aware that I'm still captive here?
I doubt you intended to hold me prisoner
And when you closed the door behind you,
I never even knew I held the key

I Am Enough

Let me introduce you
To the me I've come to know
Someone I'm reminded of
When life deals a fateful blow
Sometimes I may lose
And others I might win
But it doesn't really matter if
I'm comfortable in my skin

Life isn't always easy
And the road at times feels rough
It's easy to feel on top of the world
When you're standing on marshmallow fluff

The challenge is to love yourself
When walls are caving in
No one can't put you on a shelf
If validation comes from within

When others disappoint me
I say that I am enough
And if the world rejects me
I feel that I am enough
Left alone in solitude
I know that I am enough
God makes no mistakes, you see
And it's simply enough to just be me
Now that I know who I truly am
It feels so damn good to be free

ANIMALS
&
NATURE

Lightsome Things

(From the poem "Butterflies Are Lightsome Things" by Xi Xi (part of line 19 and line 21), as translated from the Chinese by Jennifer Feeley)

Cuz butterflies are lightsome things,
My heart **flutters by** with an arduous cadence—
Zing! Zang! Zip!
Whenever they are near
The ominous kaleidoscope of airy-fairy wings
Stops breath in its tracks—*pfft!*
Which way will they go?
Where do they land when they
Grow weary of their lofty voyage?
Let it be me! Let it be me!
I'll hold my breath like a corpse
My statuesque chassis will cement to the earth
Like a one-hundred-year-old cypress
You don't see me! You don't see me!

It's safe to usurp
You're in neutral territory here,
Like a Swiss Alp
Or an alabaster litmus paper
The prospect of a celestial visitor
Weighs on my mind like a hefty lead lure
I think I'll sit on this bench and
Rest. Just Rest.

The rhythmic beat of my heart returns like a metronome
Breath now ebbs and flows with the cadence of a dutiful soldier
Thoughts rifle through a checklist
Of should-haves, would-haves, and could-haves and
I don't even notice the imperial monarch resting on my hand
There is little danger of abdication

The Stargazing Cat

(Inspired by the poem "The Cat in the Forbidden City
Gazes at Stars" by Xi Xi, as translated from the Chinese
by Jennifer Feeley)

The ginormous tabby tilts his head to the heavens
He must be the weight of a pig or, at least, a wolverine
His emerald eyes sink into tiny slits of origami
And contract as he ogles the starry night tableau
Golden-amber hues shimmer in his peripheral
Like lofty, fall leaves amidst a subtle breeze

His stoic silhouette exudes the confidence of a soldier
Cats are said to be guardians of the spiritual realm
My soul is a precious gemstone naked and raw
In need of protection like an unshucked oyster,
my pearl is tucked neatly out of sight

I would pay a pittance to learn his observations:
Does the feline gaze at Pisces?
A fish out of reach still makes the mind wander
And the tongue salivate
Maybe the cheese-cloaked moon
Is the reason his motor never idles?
Or perhaps he communes with his ancestors
Who knowingly twinkle at Earth's slumber?
Their twilight seems like an invitation
For those cloaked in the veil of night
To look upward and ponder more light

But the fat cat already knows
He has pondered all the while
He is my spirit animal—
My bridge between this world
And the one(s) in the ether(s)
Waiting to pounce
On those who disregard
The importance of
Fa
fal
fall
falli
fallin
falling
STARS

Alaska

I.

Hidden in your mountain's bosom
We suckle the fruit of the elderberry
Stumble upon fool's gold or shimmering quartz
In your green lichened forest
We meditate with lucid waterfalls and
Thirstily drink from your chattering streams

II.

A trail of wild raspberries,
Is an invitation to your wooded splendor
As a salmon jumping playfully is a temptress to the bear
Majestic, umbrella-like plants shelter a teary night
As I dread the ferry home

III.

On the pier, a sea otter sidles by
Nosily poking his whiskered head about—
A quiet spectator blending subtly with night
And the eagle so magnificent and cool
Glides across the water landing dinner for two
From the shore, I envy its clever shrewdness

IV.

Starfish clinging fervently to the pier
Are barnacles of calloused beauty
A translucent jellyfish contracts in the water—
Like me, this ghost rider, makes its ceaseless journey home

Clear and amiable I scoop it up
Admiring its delicate features
I see that it's a flowering luminary,
Beautiful like Monet's Water Lilies
One more caress as it slips into the sea,
An apparition of childlike wonder
This is Alaska—
The final frontier, the first in beauty

Forget-Me-Not

It doesn't have to mean everything—
Only something

Something more than nothing
Nothing more than something

Don't want a bouquet of roses
A simple forget-me-not will do

Don't want a handful of promises
Just a little piece of you

So remember just this one thing:
It doesn't have to mean everything—
Only something

Rain Vows

Got married to the rain today
I reared back my head,
Captured her on my tongue
And consummated my love
While citing vows of adulation
Before the stars, the moon,
And a river called loneliness
Wildflower girls strewed an array of petals
Adorning festive wreaths on their heads
Squirrels were sprightly ring bearers
Spilling acorns from their teeming pockets
As they waltzed on an altar of driftwood
The morels all spore witness to the gleeful event
And the leaves were animated guests casting
Plethoras of colorful toasts to the betrothed

I'm enamored with rain
She reminds me that life
Is a gift, and that there's no
Time like the present
To nurture our dreams
She cleanses my impurities
And washes away years
Of scorn and avarice
I get carried away in the rain—
Love to bask. Love to play
It's a match made in heaven
A bond never to be broken
Until the sun arrives to crash the party
Or someone opens their umbrella

Delicate Flowers

We are all just delicate flowers
Each of us has an aesthetic unique to ourselves
But we depend on each other to communicate and thrive
And without rain, we could not understand rainbows
Without gales, we could not comprehend
Calm and tranquility. We weather
Raging storms and suffer
Unthinkable loss so that
With time and resilience
We can find the sun
Though some of our lustrous petals may wilt and stems break
The wind will carry our seeds of doubt to gentler breezes
Where we
Can scatter
And start
Over with
A renewed
Hope and
Although
We may
Lose some
Of our
Precious
Features,
Our essence
Remains flawless

ENDINGS
&
BEGINNINGS

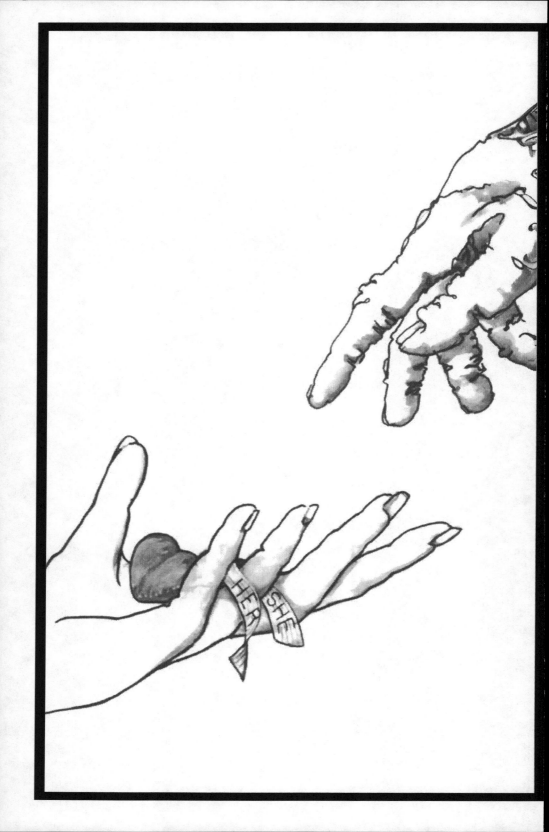

Chocolate Makes Her Feel Better

She is a ripened peach fighting fermentation
An untied hospital gown fashions crevices once called skin
Her wrinkles are storytellers weary from too much history:
Tales of The Great Depression, theater, and Handel escape
from each pore and penetrate my soul
"You know, I vomited," she whispers,
"—Just wouldn't stay in me."
"I know." I mutter as I squeeze her delicate hand

The cancer spreads faster now
Her malignant cells are rabid wolves
hungrily devouring her peanut-brittle body
Her memory, once sharp, is dull and less resilient
As she awaits her death like a welcome friend

In her earlier days, we spoke of playwrights
And what Hitler had done to her heritage
We ate matzo and sang Phantom of the Opera
As I brushed the hair of a venerable princess

I repress the tears a hospice worker
Doesn't feel the right to show
My heart is heavy and my tongue thick
I search for words that might have meaning. . .
"Is there anything in the world I can get you? Anything at all?"
She contemplates, and the gears churn in her archaic mind
Her thoughts are interrupted by a pattering of pain
She grimaces, shifts, and breathes deep
Each word is a calculated soldier marching bravely to the front lines

"Hmm, yes—chocolate. . .
I think chocolate would make me feel better
Just plain old-fashioned milk chocolate."

When I return from the store the bed is empty
This time, I don't shun the tears that overstay
Their welcome like uninvited houseguests
My life forever touched, I head for the door
grateful for my once thought "complacent" life

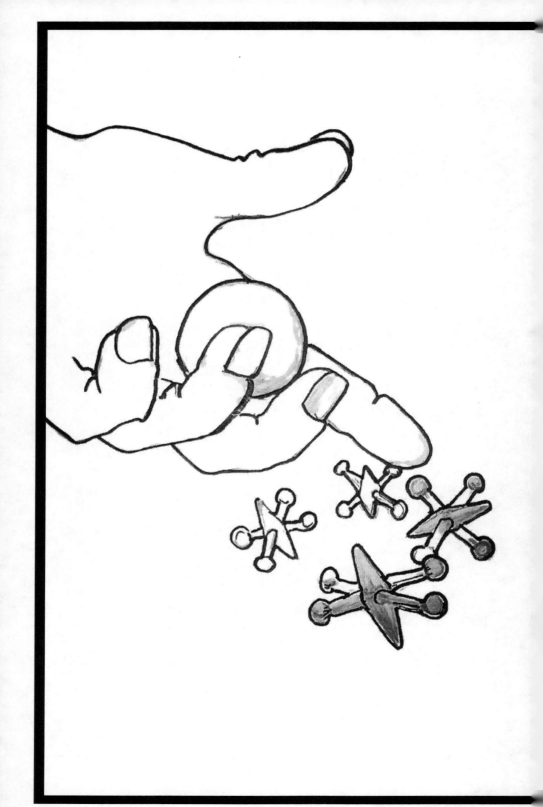

The Recycling
For J.P. [1957—2010]

Your intelligence was bigger than the world
The world brought disappointment
Disappointment was a trusted friend—
A friend to rejection
Rejection unfeeling
Feeling unloved
Love, an elusive dream
You dream no more
No more hope
Hope extinguished
Extinguished life
Life is a game—

GAME
OVER

Will you play again?

Ghosts

You drifted into my life
A phantasmic apparition of wonder
Drained the moat, chiseled the
Fortress around this heart,
And rolled me in like thunder
Then crumble, crumble,
These walls took a tumble
And a stealthy grim reaper
Harvested my soul amidst the rubble
Kindred specters emerged from the night
And took to the flame like moths to a light
Synchronicities astounded
But your love for another was bounded
I won't be anyone's concubine
I'm worthy of a love completely mine
I wouldn't let it get that far
I'm not in the habit of collecting scars
So my honesty spooked you, shit got real
I made you feel things that you didn't want to feel
And now you ghost me, ghost me
Light your candle and roast me
Like a poltergeist you consumed me til' I gave you a fright
Then you cut the rope, loosened your grip,
And released me back into the night
So, you placed me like flotsam
In the attic of your mind
The hunt made you thirsty but the quench didn't bind
You built a monster fortress
to protect your phantom heart

The brick and mortar were cemented
And gave us time apart
And now you ghost me, ghost me
Light your candle and roast me
Not gonna let this hurt me
I've been through much worse
What started as a blessing has now become a curse
I always knew it would come down to choice
And that my straw was paper thin
I kept my cool as long as I could
I struggled to let you in
You set me up with another
So you wouldn't have to face
Your own heart
But I'm no stray dog in need of rescue
I was enough from the start
There's a difference between
Loneliness and being alone
And I'm quite capable on my own
So, now I'll ghost you, roast you
Light my candle and toast you
And scatter you like ashes
In the catacombs of my mind
I'll leave you a remnant
Of naïve sentiment
A silent wraith
That's hard to erase,
You're nothing but a haunting revenant
I'll light some sage to cleanse my space

A Breath of Fresh Air

A talent with muted passion
You make me feel free to be me

A fish out of water—
A foreigner in my own country
You make me feel free to be me

Loved by many, yet misunderstood
You make me feel free to be me
You simply allow me to be. . .
F R E E!

union

(Edward Estlin Cummings in memoriam)

you can put the man in wo(man)
and the he in s(he)
you can put the male in fe(male)
but you can't put him in her

and thus, without one, we are no one
and with one, we are not al(one)

hers isn't his, but he is (he)rs
are is in d(are), but is isn't daring
the (was)n't was and the (has)n't has

the us in d(us)t is the way we (we)re, but
with(in) and with(out) brings us full circle
and the here in t(here) is everyw(here)!

and to give your all is to not be (not)hing
the me in (me)mory is who i re(me)mber
and so I smile at the warmth of december
for in its end(in)g.
is also its beg(in)n(in)g. . .

Baby's Breath

God whispered you into my womb
From his big hands grew tiny fingers

How quickly my love for you did bloom
And still, it always lingers

From angel wings to baby's breath
You danced into my heart

A bond so true not even death
Can pull the two apart

Contributor Bios

Lynette Feeley is an Interlochen Arts Academy and The University of Michigan graduate, poet, writer, and editor who lives in the Midwest with her family and rescue cat, Simba. She wrote a TV show that was considered for development by Creative Artists Agency and wrote several screenplays plays that all placed at various levels (as high as fifth place) in film competitions. Her poetry was previously published in Writers' Journal and The University of Michigan—Dearborn's Lyceum The Literary & Fine Arts Journal. This is her first poetry collection. She is currently working on her debut novel.

Carol Gazso Kushion is a visual artist, instrumental musician, and vocal artist. She graduated from Central Michigan University with a Bachelor of Music Education (B.M.E.) degree in 1976. After graduating, Ms. Kushion devoted three decades to teaching and directing in Michigan public schools. Retired from public education, she divides her creative time between performing and visual arts. Currently, Ms. Kushion is an affiliate of Tawas Bay Art Gallery, where her work is on display. She and her husband Alan reside with their chocolate lab Berkeley on Tawas Lake in the Tawas Bay Area in northeast lower Michigan.

Author Photo Credit: Edward Bloom

Made in United States
Orlando, FL
14 November 2023

38943825R00050